IT'S TIME TO EAT PEPPERMINT COOKIES

It's Time to Eat PEPPERMINT COOKIES

Walter the Educator

Silent King Books
A WhichHead Entertainment Imprint

Copyright © 2025 by Walter the Educator

All rights reserved. No part of this book may be reproduced in any manner whatsoever without written per- mission except in the case of brief quotations embodied in critical articles and reviews.

First Printing, 2024

Disclaimer

This book is a literary work; the story is not about specific persons, locations, situations, and/or circumstances unless mentioned in a historical context. Any resemblance to real persons, locations, situations, and/or circumstances is coincidental. This book is for entertainment and informational purposes only. The author and publisher offer this information without warranties expressed or implied. No matter the grounds, neither the author nor the publisher will be accountable for any losses, injuries, or other damages caused by the reader's use of this book. The use of this book acknowledges an understanding and acceptance of this disclaimer.

It's Time to Eat PEPPERMINT COOKIES is a collectible early learning book by Walter the Educator suitable for all ages belonging to Walter the Educator's Time to Eat Book Series. Collect more books at WaltertheEducator.com

USE THE EXTRA SPACE TO TAKE NOTES AND DOCUMENT YOUR MEMORIES

PEPPERMINT COOKIES

The oven beeps, oh, what a treat!

It's Time to Eat
Peppermint Cookies

It's time for something warm and sweet.

A special snack, so crisp and bright,

Peppermint cookies, pure delight!

The smell drifts softly through the air,

A hint of mint is everywhere.

With sugar sprinkles, red and white,

They sparkle in the kitchen light.

Careful now, they're way too hot!

We'll wait a bit, just not a lot!

A glass of milk is standing by,

For when they're cool and not too dry.

Pick one up, but take it slow,

A little nibble, there you go!

Crunchy, minty, oh so yum!

Hooray, hooray, the time has come!

It's Time to Eat
Peppermint Cookies

One big bite, a happy grin,

The best of treats to share with kin.

Crispy edges, soft inside,

With candy swirls that shine with pride!

Grandma smiles and takes a bite,

Mom and Dad say, "What a sight!"

A plate of cookies, round and neat,

So many hands, so many feet!

The crumbs all dance across the floor,

Someone says, "Can we have more?"

One for you and one for me,

Sharing treats is fun, you see!

The plate gets empty, what a shame,

But baking more is just a game!

We'll mix and roll and bake again,

It's Time to Eat
Peppermint Cookies

With peppermint swirls that never end!

Time to clean, let's wipe and sweep,

The kitchen's sparkling, fresh and neat.

With happy hearts, we all agree,

What fun today has come to be!

So when you smell that minty cheer,

You'll know that cookie time is near!

Gather 'round, both big and small,

It's Time to Eat
Peppermint Cookies

Peppermint cookies, best of all!

ABOUT THE CREATOR

Walter the Educator is one of the pseudonyms for Walter Anderson. Formally educated in Chemistry, Business, and Education, he is an educator, an author, a diverse entrepreneur, and he is the son of a disabled war veteran. "Walter the Educator" shares his time between educating and creating. He holds interests and owns several creative projects that entertain, enlighten, enhance, and educate, hoping to inspire and motivate you. Follow, find new works, and stay up to date with Walter the Educator™

at WaltertheEducator.com

www.ingramcontent.com/pod-product-compliance
Lightning Source LLC
LaVergne TN
LVHW052013060526
838201LV00059B/4020